Crete Public Library
305 East 13th St.
Crete, NE 68333
Established 1878

W9-BZV-203

Who Grows Up in the Ocean?

A Book About Ocean Animals and Their Offspring

Written by Theresa Longenecker
Illustrated by Melissa Carpenter

Content Advisor: Julie Dunlap, Ph.D.
Reading Advisor: Lauren A. Liang, M.A.
Literacy Education, University of Minnesota
Minneapolis, Minnesota

PiCTURE WiNDOW BOOKS
Minneapolis, Minnesota

PUBLIC LIBRARY
CRETE, NEBRASKA

Editor: Peggy Henrikson
Designer: Melissa Voda
Page production: The Design Lab
The illustrations in this book were prepared digitally.

Picture Window Books
5115 Excelsior Boulevard
Suite 232
Minneapolis, MN 55416
1-877-845-8392
www.picturewindowbooks.com

Copyright © 2003 by Picture Window Books
All rights reserved. No part of this book may be reproduced without written permission from the publisher.
The publisher takes no responsibility for the use of any of the materials or methods described in this book,
nor for the products thereof.

Printed in the United States of America.

Library of Congress Cataloging-in-Publication Data
Longenecker, Theresa, 1955-
  Who grows up in the ocean? : a book about ocean animals and their offspring / written by Theresa
Longenecker ; illustrated by Melissa Carpenter.
    p. cm.
  Summary: Describes animal babies found in the ocean, including young dolphins, moon jellies, and
seahorses.
  ISBN 1-4048-0026-3 (lib. bdg. : alk. paper)
  1. Marine animals—Infancy—Juvenile literature. [1. Marine animals. 2. Animals—Infancy.]
I. Carpenter, Melissa, ill. II. Title.
  QL122.2 .L66 2003
  591.3'9—dc21
                                                                                              2002006290

591.3 C ★
Longnecker
Ingram 26.26
12/11/04

Oceans cover most of the earth. Many baby animals grow up in oceans around the world.

Some ocean babies need to breathe air. Others can breathe in the water. Some babies are raised by their parents. Others take care of themselves.

Let's read about some of the animals that grow up in the ocean.

Seahorse young

Baby Atlantic lined seahorses are called seahorse young.

Seahorse young hatch from eggs. The father seahorse carries the eggs in a pouch. After they hatch, the seahorse young swim out of the pouch on their own. If they don't, their father's pouch tightens and squirts them out.

Did you know?
Some kinds of seahorses can have 650 young at one time.

Calf

A baby blue whale is called a calf.

Imagine drinking 800 glasses of milk a day! A blue whale calf drinks at least that much of its mother's milk every day. The calf stays near its mother for about one year.

Pup

A baby sea otter is called a pup.

A sea otter pup rides on its mother's chest. The mother feeds the pup and combs its thick fur with her front paws. Soon the pup will be able to swim for food.

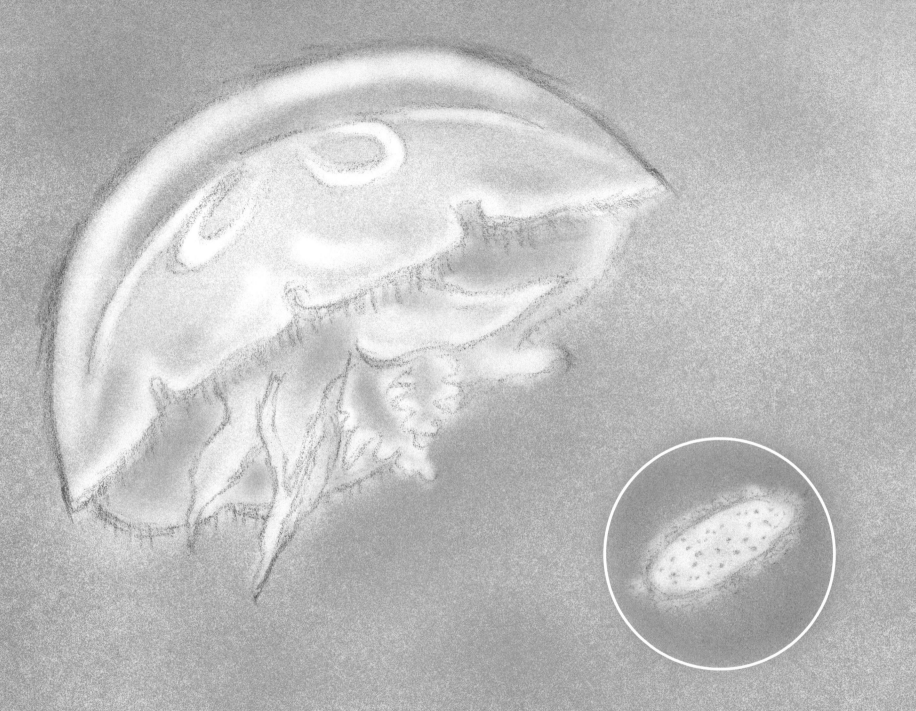

Larva

A baby moon jelly is called a larva.

After hatching, a moon jelly larva takes care of itself. The larva drifts in the sea, looking for a home. It will choose the first hard thing it can cling to, like a rock or a piece of coral.

Did you know?
When it first hatches, a moon jelly larva doesn't look anything like its parents. It's also so small that you'd need a microscope to see it.

Calf

A baby bottlenose dolphin is called a calf.

Soon after it is born, a dolphin calf begins to sink. The mother gently pushes her baby up out of the water for its first breath of air.

Did you know?
A calf talks to its mother by clicking, squeaking, and whistling.

14

Hatchling

A baby green sea turtle is called a hatchling.

Sea turtle hatchlings are on their own right from the start. The babies dig themselves out of their buried nest on the beach, then they scramble to the sea.

Did you know?
Baby sea turtles hitch a ride in floating seaweed. The tangled plants hide them from hungry birds overhead and hungry fish down below.

Pup

A baby great hammerhead shark is called a pup.

Great hammerhead shark pups are born ready to move. They swim away from their mother and are on their own. The mother shark gives birth far away from other adult sharks, who might harm the pups.

Larva

A baby American lobster is called a larva.

A newly hatched larva floats away from the mother lobster. Thousands of larvae are hatched at the same time. The larvae swim at the water surface for about 25 days. Then they sink to the bottom to feed and grow their shells.

Did you know?
A newly hatched lobster larva is about the size of a mosquito. As the larva grows, it will shed its shell 10 times in the first year alone.

Fast Facts

Atlantic Lined Seahorse: When seahorse young are born, they are often less than one-half inch (about one centimeter) long. As they grow, the bony plates in their skin harden and become like armor. Adult seahorses are almost as tall as a new pencil. They have long snouts to suck up tiny shrimp and larvae. But they have no teeth, so they swallow these creatures whole.

Blue Whale: A blue whale calf and its mother talk to each other in loud moans and groans. Some of their sounds can be heard many miles away in the ocean. At birth, a calf weighs about as much as an adult elephant. When the blue whale calf is fully grown, it will weigh as much as 30 or 40 elephants put together!

Sea Otter: A sea otter pup stays with its mother almost all the time. The mother leaves the pup only to dive for food. After about six months, the pup is ready to live on its own. Sea otters eat a lot of food—up to one-fifth of their body weight every day. An otter eats while floating on its back, using its chest like a table.

Moon Jelly: A jelly, or jellyfish, is almost all water. It has no heart, bones, or eyes. The mouth of the jelly is on its underside. It lands on top of little sea animals and eats them. A moon jelly might look beautiful floating in the water, but its long tentacles can sting. Even a dead moon jelly can sting if its tentacles are still wet.

Bottlenose Dolphin: A bottlenose dolphin calf stays with its mother for three to six years. Dolphins sometimes use body movements, such as slapping their tails on the water, to tell each other things. They dive underwater but come up every few minutes for air. A dolphin sleeps near the surface of the water so it can breathe.

Green Sea Turtle: A female green sea turtle sometimes travels thousands of miles to find the right nesting place. She lays her eggs on the same beach where she hatched over 10 years earlier. She lays 100 to 150 eggs at a time. Six to eight weeks later, the baby sea turtles hatch. A sea turtle hatchling uses a sharp bump on its nose, called an egg tooth, to break out of its shell.

Great Hammerhead Sharks: Sharks are known for their razor-sharp teeth. Great hammerhead shark pups are born with all of their teeth—six or seven rows of them! Great hammerhead sharks can tear apart and eat fish, squid, octopuses, stingrays, and even other sharks. Sharks' eyes work as well as their teeth. They need good eyesight to see in the dim light of the deep sea.

American Lobster: An American lobster larva's shell gets tight and cracks open as it grows. The larva crawls out, shedding the old shell. This shedding of its old shell is called molting. The shell underneath then hardens and becomes a new shell. Lobsters molt many times as they grow. Slowly, they begin to look like their parents.

Ocean Babies at a Glance

Word for Baby	Animal	Born How	First Food	Word for Group
Young	Seahorse	Egg	Small, shrimp-like animals	———
Calf	Blue whale	Live	Mother's milk	Pod, school, grind
Pup	Sea otter	Live	Mother's milk	Herd
Larva	Moon jelly	Egg	Small, shrimp-like animals	Smack
Calf	Dolphin	Live	Mother's milk	Pod, school, herd
Hatchling	Sea turtle	Egg	Tiny sea animals	Bale
Pup	Shark	Live	Small fish	School, shiver
Larva	Lobster	Egg	Small, shrimp-like animals	———

Where Do They Live?

Atlantic lined seahorse—the western Atlantic from Nova Scotia to Argentina, and the Gulf of Mexico

Blue whale—deep parts of oceans all over the world

Sea otter—near the shores of the northern Pacific Ocean

Moon jelly—tropical waters and oceans with mild temperatures worldwide

Bottlenose dolphin—oceans worldwide except around the poles, often near land

Green sea turtle—tropical and warm oceans worldwide

Great hammerhead shark—tropical and warm oceans worldwide

American lobster—northwestern Atlantic Ocean from Labrador to North Carolina, usually in cold or cool waters on rocky seafloors

Make an Ocean Puzzle

What You Need

A sheet of drawing paper

Markers or crayons

A sheet of thin cardboard the same size as the paper

Glue

Scissors

What to Do

1. Think about some of your favorite ocean animals and their babies.
2. Draw a picture of the ocean. Show the water, the top of the water, and a bit of blue sky above the water. Add your animals with their babies. Draw them where you think they belong. Do they usually live near the ocean floor, around the middle, or near the top of the water?
3. Add rocks and sea plants to the ocean floor. You might want to draw floating seaweed in the water or birds in the sky.
4. Glue your picture to the cardboard and let it dry.
5. Cut your ocean picture into puzzle pieces, making each animal one piece.
6. Now give your puzzle to someone else and see if they can figure out where your ocean animals belong. Soon they'll see your whole ocean picture!

Words to Know

egg tooth—a sharp bump on top of an animal's nose or beak, used to break out of an egg

hatch—to break out of an egg

hatchling—a newly hatched animal

larva—an animal in the stage of growth between hatching and adulthood. *Larvae* (LAR-vee) means more than one larva.

microscope—a tool that scientists use to make very small things look bigger

molting—when an animal's outer covering comes off so a new one can grow

shed—to drop or fall off

snout—the long, front part of an animal's head that includes its nose, jaws, and mouth

tentacle—a long, flexible limb (like a leg or an arm), used for moving, feeling, and grabbing. Moon jellies have tentacles.

To Learn More

At the Library

Bair, Diane, and Pamela Wright. *Whale Watching.* Mankato, Minn.: Capstone Press, 2000.

Gray, Samantha. *Ocean.* New York: Dorling Kindersley Pub., 2001.

Nathan, Emma. *What Do You Call a Baby Crab?: And Other Baby Fish and Ocean Creatures.* Woodbridge, Conn.: Blackbirch Press, 1999.

FactHound

FactHound offers a safe, fun way to find Web sites related to this book. All of the sites on FactHound have been researched by our staff.
www.facthound.com

1. Visit the FactHound home page.

2. Enter a search word related to this book, or type in this special code: 1404800263.

3. Click the FETCH IT button.

Your trusty FactHound will fetch the best Web sites for you!

Index

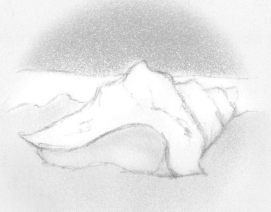